Date Due

EPSTEIN DRAWINGS

Scottish Landscape. Pastel, 1957

EPSTEIN DRAWINGS

With notes by
LADY EPSTEIN

and an introduction by
RICHARD BUCKLE

THE WORLD PUBLISHING COMPANY
CLEVELAND AND NEW YORK

Published by The World Publishing Company
2231 West 110th Street, Cleveland 2, Ohio

FIRST EDITION

133175

CONTENTS

7

INTRODUCTION

A number of books could be made of Epstein's drawings and watercolours: a book of portraits, or one devoted solely to his portraits of children; a book of nude studies from life, or books made up exclusively of single series of studies—such as the 'Indian Sisters' or 'Indian Mother and Child'*; a collection of his flower pieces or his landscapes of Epping Forest; editions of the Old Testament or of Baudelaire's *Fleurs du Mal* with his copious illustrations to them; or, perhaps most interesting of all, an assembly of his drawings for sculpture. All these could and should be published. The fact that every aspect of his graphic work is illustrated in the present volume, that portraits, nudes, studies for sculpture and book illustrations are all mixed together, may seem to deprive the collection of unity, yet unity it has, and one of a very special kind: for all the drawings illustrated here are from the collection of the sculptor's wife.

For many years Lady Epstein was the constant witness of the sculptor's work, discussing with him everything he did, occasionally venturing a criticism—the only person, possibly, ever to do so; and from being the most regular student of the master's sculpture and drawings became, in the natural course of events, the greatest expert on them. It follows that any drawing he gave her would be given for a special purpose: either that it was the best of a batch, or had some particular quality they both admired; or that it was unique—the only scribble made in preparation for carving a monument; or that it was the project for some unrealised sculpture; or it might be a rare sketch surviving from an early period, all other traces of which had been dispersed or destroyed. In fact, most of these are early works, over half having been made before the end of the first war. Kathleen Epstein has herself written the notes on the drawings from her collection.

Epstein, of course, drew long before he sculpted. He was largely self-taught, though in his 'teens he attended for a term or two one of New York's few art schools. When his family moved from the Jewish quarter in Lower East Side Manhattan, he was so attached to the characters he observed and drew in the street markets and sweat shops that he stayed behind: and from early days, he tells us in his autobiography, he could always sell his drawings. It is unfortunate that Lady Epstein's collection contains none of his remarkable studies of Ghetto types, which (influenced by the caricatures of Steinlen and Forain, and perhaps by drawings of Toulouse-Lautrec seen at Durand-Ruel's gallery on Fifth Avenue) were so much broader and bolder in style than anything else being done in America at the

*The sculptor made some hundreds of studies of the beautiful model Sunita with her sister Anita or with her son Enver.

9

turn of the century. This youthful New York period is represented by two quite different drawings, less distinctive (one being a self-portrait, No. 1), and by some curious illustrations to—or rather, variations on the theme of—Whitman's *Calamus*, dealing with the loves of boys (Nos. 3-6). Not in their style of drawing, which is extremely tentative and aims at dramatic chiaroscuro, but because of their steam-bath atmosphere, their elongations and the strange, stiff attitudes of the lovers, these suggest an influence of Aubrey Beardsley.

It was Epstein's illustrations to Horace Hapgood's *The Spirit of the Ghetto*, in which he was able to use a number of his vivid studies of the Jewish types who had first aroused his desire to draw, that paid his passage to France in 1902. The two years of his sojourn in Paris are represented by two drawings only, for the artist at this time would frequently, in a rage of dissatisfaction, destroy everything in his studio, and these are the only ones known to exist. These drawings are of the same baby whose modelled head is Epstein's earliest surviving work of sculpture.

In 1905 Epstein settled in London. Apart from a few trips to America, France and Italy, he was to remain there for life. No. 12, made soon after he came to England, is an important drawing, not only because it is his earliest study for sculpture to survive, but because the statue he modelled from it (and later destroyed) was the work which particularly aroused the enthusiasm of Charles Holden, an architect brought to Epstein by Francis Dodd, who promptly commissioned the young, unknown and desperately poor sculptor to carve the eighteen 'Strand Statues' on the new British Medical Association building. Epstein then moved from his tumble-down studio in Fulham Road to a more spacious one in Cheyne Walk. This drawing of the 'Girl with a Dove' is done in a linear style reminiscent of Gauguin; and there is about it something of Art Nouveau and such eighteen-ninetyish illustrators as Charles Ricketts. Of course, the *way* it was drawn would not affect the way the sculpture turned out: what must have survived in the modelled figure was the mixture of lyrical and monumental, of Western grace combined with something hieratic derived from a study of Egyptian, Indian and African sculpture. The lack of daintiness and sentiment must have been quite startling to amateurs of such sculpture as there was in Edwardian England.

Of the several sketches for Strand Statues here included, only one, No. 15, a study for the ninth statue from the left, the 'Mother and Child', is almost exactly as the carving turned out. (In the drawing the Mother lacks her baby, and in the resulting sculpture her pregnancy was put back a month or two). Other preliminary jottings for monumental works, some mere scribbles, some close to the realised sculpture, are those for the 'Maternity' of 1910 (Nos. 18 and 19), a carving never finished, the Oscar Wilde tomb in Hopton Wood stone of 1910-1912 (No. 25), the 'Risen Christ' in bronze of 1918 (No. 37), the Portland stone 'Night' of 1929 (No. 46), the marble 'Genesis' of 1930 (No. 54), and the bronze 'St. Michael' of 1958 (No. 64). These are all of extreme documentary interest.

No. 20, the 'Portrait Head of a Young Girl', done about 1909, but possibly a

Introduction

year or two later, seems to herald the movement known as 'The Vortex'. Epstein returned at the end of 1912 from six months in Paris (where he had seen his Wilde tomb installed in the cemetery of Père Lachaise) full of the new ideas of Picasso, Brancusi and Modigliani; and he became a Vorticist, along with Wyndham Lewis and Gaudier-Brzeska. Vorticism was a confused doctrine, owing something both to the French Cubists and the Italian Futurists, but professing to go further than either of them. Epstein's 'Rock Drill' and his drawings for it, two of which (Nos. 31 and 32) are reproduced here, reflect the Futurist passion for machinery. His grand and simple carving in marble of two 'Doves', now in the collection of Mr. Billy Rose, but intended by its owner for the new museum of sculpture in Jerusalem, was as near as he ever got to the pure forms of Brancusi. No. 28 is a study for it. The sculptor's Vortex period, coinciding with a stay at Pett Level on the Sussex coast, lasted from 1913 till 1916. He was never to do work so nearly 'abstract' again.

Portraits and figure studies range from the sculptural head of Nan (No. 22), a favourite Gypsy model, done in 1911, and the careful drawings of her in the nude—one of which (No. 24) was almost exactly reproduced in bronze as 'The Dreamer' —to the freer drawings of Anita (No. 45) and Sunita (No. 57), done in the late 'twenties and early 'thirties, and to the leonine head of Kitty, the sculptor's second daughter, done in 1937 (No. 60). When excited by a model, Epstein would make sketch after sketch in a furious search for form. But he would also go for years on end without doing any drawings at all. It is doubtful to what extent even the most finished of his drawings from life were intended as ends in themselves. Once he had made a series, as he did of his son Jackie and of Sunita and Anita and of Sunita with her son, he could easily be persuaded that they would make an interesting exhibition. Whether a good drawing is something finished and complete in itself or something exploratory will forever be a matter for dispute. A world separates the delicate impression of 'Kathleen' (No. 48) and the studiously observed 'Negress Sleeping' (No. 61). In some of his best drawings, Epstein rivals the brilliant pencil of Augustus John; (during Epstein's early days in London, in fact, the two artists formed a drawing class in Chelsea where, for a time, they worked from the same models).

In his illustrations to the Old Testament and to Baudelaire, the sculptor gave rein to the dark, visionary aspect of his genius which produced such extraordinary carvings as 'Jacob and the Angel' and 'Lazarus'. Some students will be repelled by the violence and crudity of such images as No. 51, 'The Spirit moving on the Waters', or No. 62, 'La Fontaine de Sang': others will see in them a grandeur of imagination comparable to Fuseli or Blake.

Will Epstein be remembered and extolled more for his portrait heads or for the mysterious great carvings which aroused such controversy during his life? Or for monumental castings such as the Cavendish Square 'Madonna and Child' and the Llandaff 'Christ in Majesty' which fall half-way between? The two sides of his

Introduction

character, the devoted humanist who modelled the heads of Esther and 'The Sick Child', and the thundering prophet who hacked 'Night' and 'Day' and 'Adam' from vast blocks of stone, are both represented by the very diverse drawings in this volume. But, of course, it is to Epstein's sculpture we must turn to take his true measure; and a comprehensive survey of it is in preparation. This book is really a footnote which the hazards of publishing have promoted to the rank of an overture.

RICHARD BUCKLE

NOTES ON THE PLATES

1. SELF PORTRAIT *(Red Chalk)* 1901
$12'' \times 9\frac{1}{16}''$

The only self-portrait drawing, though the artist modelled two heads of himself; one in 1912 and the other in 1920. The first is now in the National Portrait Gallery. It is interesting to compare Augustus John's study of the same subject in the same medium but done several years later. This also is in the National Portrait Gallery.

2. CHILDREN RESTING 1901
$9\frac{1}{16}'' \times 12''$

Slight though it is, this sketch is interesting as being one of the early New York period before the artist came to Europe. It also reveals his early interest in the movement of children which remained all through his life. His earliest portrait head to survive was of a new-born babe and his last work, the Bowater House Group for Hyde Park, contains the figure of a child in robust movement.

3, 4, 5, 6. ILLUSTRATIONS TO WHITMAN'S *CALAMUS*
(Pen and Ink and Wash) 1901
(3) $9\frac{1}{8}'' \times 14\frac{1}{4}''$; (4) $12\frac{1}{4}'' \times 8''$; (5) $14\frac{1}{4}'' \times 9''$; (6) $12\frac{1}{4}'' \times 8''$

This series (I believe there were originally twelve) was based on Whitman's poem of this name. When Epstein was about sixteen he attended a centre in New York called the Community Guild where a man named Paulding read Whitman and Ruskin aloud. This was his introduction to the poet whose influence was to remain with him all his life. These were the drawings he showed to Bernard Shaw when he first came to England, after which visit Shaw wrote to a friend saying he thought the world would hear more of this young man. I can find nothing in later work at all corresponding in technique or physical type with these early drawings. At no other period did he illustrate Whitman, though some years ago he was asked by a member of the Whitman Society in Detroit to make a bronze portrait of him, with the idea of placing it in Poets Corner, Westminster Abbey. Permission for this was not sanctioned, but any disappointment on this score was more than compensated for by the commission in 1957 to model the Blake bust for Poet's Corner, where it now stands.

7, 8. STUDIES OF A NEW-BORN BABE *(Pen and Ink)* 1904
(7) $18\frac{3}{4}'' \times 12\frac{1}{8}''$; (8) $15\frac{1}{4}'' \times 12\frac{1}{4}''$

In 1904 a model came to the Paris studio asking for work, but the sculptor's attention was drawn to the new-born baby she was holding and he made these pen and ink drawings. These were to be the starting point of the vast series of men's, women's and children's portraits which occupied a great part of the subsequent fifty years of incessant work. From the same baby he also made a life-sized head and figure for bronze.

9. PROFILE HEAD OF WOMAN (*Pencil*) 1906
$11\frac{5}{8}'' \times 8\frac{3}{4}''$

This and the following drawing are from an unknown sitter. It is interesting to see how closely and faithfully Epstein drew at this period and to what discipline he subjected himself before developing a bolder and more sculptural technique.

10. WOMAN RESTING HEAD ON HANDS (*Pencil*) 1906
$15\frac{1}{2}'' \times 11''$

See note on No. 9.

11. PROFILE OF YOUNG GIRL (*Pencil*) 1906
$19\frac{1}{8}'' \times 12\frac{3}{8}''$

This is the first of the early drawings to show any degree of stylization.

12. GIRL WITH A DOVE (*Pencil on Cardboard*) 1906
$19\frac{3}{4}'' \times 9\frac{3}{8}''$

About 1906 Epstein made a very finished life-size figure in clay of a twelve year old girl holding a bird, and it was this statue which pleased the architect Charles Holden and led to his giving Epstein the commission for the eighteen 'Strand Statues' on the British Medical Association building. At this period the sculptor destroyed many of his works in an unaccustomed mood of despair. Later he regretted this and often spoke of this particular statue, wishing he had kept it. He said an artist can only look with appreciation at his own work after years have detached him from it. Here is the original study for the destroyed work.

13. MOTHER AND CHILD (*Pencil*) 1907
$20'' \times 14''$

This drawing, in spite of its extremely delicate line and modelling, is more sculptural than any previous work and though not used for one of the Strand statues it was made with this in mind.

14. HYGEIA, STRAND FIGURE (*Charcoal and Wash*) 1907
$14\frac{5}{8}'' \times 9\frac{3}{8}''$

The first idea for a dancing girl modelled by the sculptor. From the plaster cast he made from her he carved two 'Strand Statues,' one with body turned to the spectator, the other in profile. When we see this drawing on entirely classical lines we can only wonder the more at the wave of fury that greeted these works on their completion. Something of this feeling of iconoclasm must surely have survived, for eventually on the grounds of public safety the statues were virtually destroyed. Casts of one or two of the figures taken at the instigation of Sir Muirhead Bone before demolishing show completely intact statues with no sign of crumbling.

15. MOTHER AND CHILD, STRAND STATUE (*Pen and Pencil*) 1907
20″ × 13¾″

A finished drawing for one of the Strand carvings. The word Parvati is written, but not in the artist's hand, in the right-hand corner. Certainly in its calm voluptuousness it evokes images of some Hindu goddess. It is interesting to notice the pen and ink line used to strengthen the outline of back and head, leaving the features and body to blossom in the more delicate pencil medium.

16. PHILOSOPHER. STUDIES FOR STRAND STATUE (*Pencil*) 1907
15¼″ × 21″

Here are two much slighter sketches for a Strand statue—this time a philosopher holding a winged skull, the symbol of human thought. When the figures were carved it was a young man, however, who held the skull. The sculptor used this theme of a man regarding a skull after an interval of fifty years as one of the figures in a study for a silver mace head, commissioned but never finished, for Singapore. It also occurs in one of his illustrations to Baudelaire ('Je suis comme le roi d'un pays pluvieux'). I include two versions of this sketch to show the development of the head in the second.

17. PROFILE HEAD, HAND AND ARM (*Pencil on Cardboard*) 1909
25½″ × 29½″

This and two subsequent drawings were discarded for years in a damp and dirty cellar from which I rescued them, covered in cobwebs. I think they are important as showing the artist's development and early discipline which enabled him later to work with fluency and confidence. All his sculpture was based on his early mastery of drawing. The profile head has an almost Buddha-like calm which seems to impose itself on the observer.

18. HANDS AND ARMS (*Pencil on Cardboard*) 1910
16″ × 30″

These almost vanished hands are precious as being a study for 'Maternity,' which the sculptor began in 1910, but never finished. Their protective nature is at once apparent. In the statue they are placed over the unborn child, a gesture which is repeated in a study from life of a pregnant negress, 1938. (No. 61).

19. STUDY FOR SCULPTURE, MATERNITY (*Pencil*) 1910
32″ × 22½″

Another study for 'Maternity,' this is a sculptor's working drawing, originally squared up for enlarging.

20. PORTRAIT HEAD OF A YOUNG GIRL (*Pencil*) 1909
    26" × 20"

A new technique is employed here. Stylism is combined with the very definite personal idiom of the model.

21. PORTRAIT HEAD OF LITTLE GIRL (*Pencil*) 1909
    $16\frac{1}{4}$" × $11\frac{1}{2}$"

This head suggesting great simplicity is actually drawn with much nuance and delicate observation. It is full of tenderness and suggests a bud about to blossom into flower.

22. HEAD OF NAN (*Pencil*) 1909
    20" × $13\frac{3}{4}$"

Though this drawing was a portrait of Nan Condron, a gypsy from whom Epstein worked for several years, it is extremely sculptural. There is a bust of her in the Tate Gallery.

23. TWO NUDES OF NAN (*Pencil*) 1911
    14" × 20"

The same model as Nos. 22 and 24.

24. NAN. SEATED NUDE (*Pencil*) 1911
    20" × 14"

A small bronze figure of Nan in the same pose as in this sketch was lent from the Evill Collection to the Leicester Galleries Memorial Exhibition (1960) and to the Edinburgh Festival Memorial Exhibition (1961), under the title of The Dreamer.

25. SKETCH FOR OSCAR WILDE TOMB (*Pencil*) 1909
    20" × 15"

The first study for the Oscar Wilde Tomb in Père Lachaise Cemetery, Paris, and one of two extant. The artist seems to have listed ten deadly sins instead of the usual seven and in the right hand lower corner in almost illegible script he indicates "sins for inset in double crown". The tomb was executed over a period of two and a half years and when finished it was on view to the public in the sculptor's studio on Chelsea Embankment. Crowds would come in the afternoons to see it. When it was finally set up in the Paris cemetery the French officials objected to the depicting of the naked male figure and covered it with a tarpaulin. Now nobody bothers and it is listed as being of public interest in the cemetery records.

26. THE FLAME OF LIFE (*Pencil and Wash on Board*) 1910
    $23\frac{3}{8}$" × $17\frac{1}{4}$"

In common with many artists of that period Epstein came under the influence of Puvis de Chavannes, and though it was very temporary he never lost his respect for him. I think this is the influence apparent in this drawing which was a study for a youthful project he never realised. He planned to make a very ambitious Sun Temple with many figures and at the same time he envisaged a Temple of Love with groups of lovers. He actually modelled very closely one such life size group in Paris, but he destroyed it together with a great deal of other work.

27. VORTICIST COMPOSITIONS (*Pencil and Chalk*) 1912
$18'' \times 23''$

A page of unrelated designs. The indication of two birds is interesting as foreshadowing the three marble groups of birds that came later.

28. SKETCH OF DOVES (*Pencil and Wash*) 1913
$22\frac{3}{4}'' \times 17\frac{5}{8}''$

Although extremely slight, this study of birds is interesting as foreshadowing again the large group of doves carved in marble. At this time the artist lived on the Sussex coast where he kept birds to work from. This interest developed, through a study of wings, into his preoccupation with angels which he drew and sculptured at intervals all through his life.

29. VORTICIST FIGURE (*Blue Chalk*) 1913
$25\frac{1}{4}'' \times 20\frac{3}{4}''$

It would be interesting to compare this with Modigliani's blue chalk caryatid drawings made about the same period. The two artists were friends and Modigliani was passionately interested in the African carvings which Epstein started to collect at that time.

30. HEAD (*Pen and Wash*) 1913
$25\frac{3}{4}'' \times 19\frac{1}{2}''$

I cannot relate this head to any other work by the artist but include it for the interesting and decorative treatment of the hair and the strongly sculptural planes of the head.

31. STUDY FOR ROCK DRILL (*Charcoal*) 1915
$27'' \times 16\frac{7}{8}''$

One of a series of this subject, preliminary studies for the bronze Rock Drill, now in the Tate Gallery. The sculptor became impatient with the actual drill on which the plaster figure stood, and so discarded the lower part of the composition. With the completion of this figure and the series of so called Vorticist drawings, Epstein's abstract period as such was over.

32. STUDY FOR ROCK DRILL: BACK VIEW (*Charcoal*) 1915
$27'' \times 17''$

See preceding note.

33. VORTICIST COMPOSITION (*Charcoal*) 1915
$27\frac{1}{8}'' \times 17''$

One of the most achieved of the drawings of this period. It shows the embryo child in the womb of the mother who is herself contained in a womb-like cave form.

34. PORTRAIT HEAD OF A GIRL (*Charcoal*) c.1916
$23'' \times 18\frac{1}{4}''$

A new and bolder technique emerges in the treatment of this head coupled with a deeper psychological observation.

35. WOUNDED SOLDIER (*Pencil*) 1918
$17\frac{1}{4}'' \times 12''$

People are always surprised when they see for the first time these drawings made in an army hospital during the 1914-18 war. They are certainly different from the sensuous and robust work the artist so often produced and quite naturally reflect the mood induced by the surroundings and circumstances.

36. ARMY NURSE (*Pencil*) 1918
$14\frac{5}{8}'' \times 10''$

See preceding note.

37. STUDY FOR CHRIST STATUE (*Pencil*) 1918
$14\frac{1}{2}'' \times 10\frac{3}{8}''$

The first evocation of the celebrated statue of the Risen Christ in bronze which was the storm centre of widespread abuse and praise when it was first exhibited in 1920. The modelled figure differs considerably from this sketch but the essential characteristic that remains is the importance of the hands. It would seem this was the first feature of the work to seize the sculptor's imagination.

38. PORTRAIT HEAD OF MEUM (*Pencil*) 1918
$18\frac{1}{2}'' \times 18''$

Several portraits in bronze exist of this sitter, notably Meum with a Fan and Mask of Meum done about the same period.

39. STUDY FOR FOUNTAIN GROUP (*Pencil*) 1918
$14'' \times 20''$

In spite of its precarious state and partial obliteration this drawing has been included because of its unique mythological subject matter among Epstein's drawings. Apart from two minute studies in clay of Narcissus and Pasiphae and the Bull I can think of no mythological subject executed by him in sculpture except the big Pan in his last work. All his life he wanted to make a Pan but only succeeded in achieving this immediately before he died in 1959.

40. SKETCH FOR BAS RELIEF, LOVERS (*Pencil*) 1922
    10″ × 12¾″

This drawing is barely discernible being almost obliterated by time and neglect but the essentially sculptural unity and movement remain. Having scribbled in an odd moment on the back of a box, the sculptor later thought of translating it into a marble bas relief: but the nearest he came to this was in a small bronze sketch of lovers on the back of an eagle in flight.

41. SONG OF SOLOMON (*Pencil and Wash*) 1923
    24¼″ × 18⅞″

Illustration to Chapter Two.

42. NUDE OF NEGRESS (*Pencil*) 1925
    20″ × 16⅜″

Many European artists including Grünewald, Rubens and Rembrandt liked to work from negro models. Epstein was specially interested in coloured people and used them frequently as models.

43. HEAD OF A NEGRESS (*Pencil*) 1925
    17¾″ × 24¾″

See preceding note.

44. THE BLESSING (*Pencil and Wash*) 1927
    22¾″ × 17½″

A whole scene is evoked in these few lines. The patriarch transmitting his blessing to the awed child, the mourning woman and the stillness of the desert night.

45. FIGURE STUDY, ANITA (*Pencil*) 1928
    13½″ × 17″

This time the subject is an Indian model. Later this model appears again in the long series of drawings of the Indian Sisters.

46. STUDY FOR NIGHT (*Pencil*) 1928
    22″ × 17¼″

In 1928 Epstein was commissioned to carve two stone groups over the doorways on either side of the then new Underground Building at St. James's. He seized on the idea with fervour as, apart from the small Hudson Memorial panel, it was his first architectural commission since the Wilde Tomb in 1910. These two groups are extremely massive as they seem to bear the weight of the whole building, and anything slighter would have appeared puny. The sombre maternal figure of Night lulls her weary children to sleep as they lie inert across her knees. A small maquette of the group exists in plaster.

47. HEAD OF ZEDA (*Pencil*) 1928
   $17\frac{1}{2}'' \times 13\frac{1}{8}''$

One of a series, chiefly figure drawings, made from this young Turkish model.

48. KATHLEEN (*Pencil*) 1929
   $27'' \times 21\frac{3}{4}''$

Epstein made many portraits in pencil and clay of this sitter between 1921 and 1950, the earliest bust being in the Tate Gallery.

49. THEO (*Pencil*) 1930
   $23'' \times 18\frac{1}{2}''$

Theodore Garman, painter, at the age of six.

50. NOLI ME TANGERE (*Pencil*) 1930
   $23'' \times 17\frac{1}{2}''$

Though Epstein made many illustrations for the Old Testament, this is one of the very few drawings from the Gospel. In the last year of his life he was commissioned to design twelve windows depicting the twelve apostles for a new church at Crownhill, Plymouth. Before he died he made six water-colour studies for these.

51. THE SPIRIT MOVING ON THE WATERS (*Pencil*) 1930
   $17\frac{5}{8}'' \times 22\frac{3}{4}''$

In 1930 Epstein wrote in a letter from Epping Forest 'It is raining all the time. I have nothing to read except an old bible. I keep reading Genesis and have made some drawings.' These were the first of a long series of biblical drawings which were later exhibited at the Redfern Gallery. They were all sold immediately and became so dispersed that when later on someone wanted to publish them with the text it was thought to be too great a task to trace all the owners and collect them again for reproduction, so the idea fell through.

52. THE HAND OF GOD (*Wash Drawing*) 1930
   $17\frac{1}{2}'' \times 22\frac{5}{8}''$
See preceding note.

53. JESUS AND JOHN (*Pencil and Wash*) 1930
   $24\frac{3}{4}'' \times 20''$
See note 50.

54. STUDY FOR GENESIS (*Pencil*) 1931
   $20'' \times 15''$

The only known study for the the famous marble statue of Genesis, the universal mother of mankind.

55. PIETÀ, TWO HEADS (*Pencil*) 1932
$17\frac{1}{2}'' \times 22\frac{3}{4}''$

In 1928 the sculptor was engaged with the idea of modelling a seated Pietà for which he made drawings. When he was about to embark on the work he received the commission to carve the two groups for St. James's Underground. The composition he had in mind for the Pietà was transformed and modified for the carving of Night. Later he returned to this subject and made two drawings (this and No. 56) in 1932. The two heads intended for stone carving seem already fossilised in the extremity of grief while the standing group was intended to be modelled. Although neither was carried out in sculpture these two compositions are so powerfully drawn that they seem to exist in themselves as completed works.

56. PIETÀ, TWO FIGURES (*Pencil*) 1932
$22\frac{3}{4}'' \times 17\frac{1}{2}''$

See preceding note.

57. INDIAN MOTHER AND CHILD (*Pencil*) 1932
$21\frac{1}{4}'' \times 26\frac{3}{4}''$

Epstein was always interested in exhibitions where colourful people from other countries displayed themselves and their wares. He liked describing one at the White City in long ago days, where there were whole villages inhabited by wonderful looking natives who danced and sang and worked at their crafts. With this in mind he visited Wembley World Fair and found there the beautiful Indian Sunita in charge of a stall with her younger sister and small son. These three posed for the sculptor over a period of years. Sunita could be equally a Madonna (she and her son posed for the Madonna and Child, 1926, now in a New York church) or the odalisque of many drawings—alone, with her sister, or with her boy as in the drawing here reproduced. She returned to India and died suddenly.

58. SHADRACK, MESCHAK AND ABEDNEGO (*Pencil and Wash*) 1933
$22\frac{3}{4}'' \times 17\frac{1}{2}''$

A subject of special interest to the sculptor, who wanted always to transform this drawing into sculpture but never decided on the exact medium. During the blitz of 1941, watching a tremendous fire from a Chelsea roof-top one night when a chemical factory was in flames, he reverted again to the subject of the three just men who passed unscathed through the flames. I was interested to see how an artist's mind translates every experience into the medium his mind is constantly engaged with.

59. FIGURE STUDY, MALE NUDE (*Pencil and Wash*) 1934
$17\frac{1}{4}'' \times 22\frac{1}{2}''$

A young Indian called one day to see if Epstein could use him for a model, saying it had always been his ambition to pose for him. The sculptor was engaged on portraits, but found time to make this one drawing. It is vaguely reminiscent of the Adam in

Michelangelo's Sistine ceiling. Though the pose is different there is the same long, flowing muscular line from shoulder to thigh and the same voluptuous grace.

60. PORTRAIT OF KITTY (*Pencil*) 1937
30″ × 24″

One of the artist's daughters at the age of ten. He made three portraits for bronze of the same sitter—Kitty with Curls (1944), Head of Kitty (1948) which was bought for Birmingham Art Gallery under the title of "Youth", and the large bust (1957) first exhibited in New York.

61. NEGRESS SLEEPING (*Pencil*) 1938
22″ × 26″

One of the most technically accomplished drawings here reproduced. Once again there is the recurring theme of the mother's protective hand on the unborn child, this time drawn from life. This model later posed for the mother in African Mother and Child, a bronze group now in Sturgis Ingersoll's garden collection of contemporary sculpture in Philadelphia.

62. ILLUSTRATION FOR BAUDELAIRE. *LA FONTAINE DE SANG (Pencil)* 1939
30″ × 24″

Epstein always had a profound admiration for Baudelaire's poems and when he was commissioned by the Limited Editions Club to make illustrations for their publication of these poems he was delighted and set about it with characteristic concentration. He went to Paris to steep himself in the atmosphere of the city where they were written and made many small sketches of streets and bridges where the poet walked. He came back with at least half-a-dozen copies of the 'Fleurs du Mal', so that wherever he happened to find himself there was always a volume to be brooded over at any hour of the day or night. The poems he chose to illustrate he knew by heart and he also read various lives of the poet. He set out to make very finished pencil drawings that would have the quality of steel engravings such as might have been used for illustrations of that period. He worked about six months on this series and later they were exhibited at Tooth's Gallery in 1939. Very few sold and they received very bad notices, most of them returning to the studio. The artist valued these works highly and could not understand that people shrank from the grim subject matter depicted. Although the drawings were harshly criticised and neglected, he never regretted having made them or the opportunity it gave him to study Baudelaire so intensively. The lines illustrated here start:

   ' Il me semble parfois que mon sang coule à flots
   Ainsi qu'une fontaine aux rythmiques sanglots'.

63. LUCIFER AND HIS ANGELS (*Pencil and Wash*) 1944
17⅜″ × 22¾″

Epstein made an intense study of Milton's 'Paradise Lost' and gave a great deal of thought to this subject. In this drawing the Lucifer head is more or less a self-portrait while the angel on his right became the bronze Lucifer now in Birmingham Art Gallery. Almost unknown among the sculptor's works is a bas relief of the revolt of the angels.

64. STUDY FOR ST. MICHAEL TORSO (*Pen and Pencil*) 1957
$21'' \times 16\frac{1}{4}''$

This fragment, certainly never intended for reproduction, was a studio working sketch for details of drapery for the large St. Michael figure in bronze now on Coventry Cathedral. I include it as being the last Epstein drawing as such, though later in the same year he made pastels of landscape in the Scottish Highlands.

1. Self Portrait. 1901

2. Children Resting. 1901

3. Illustration to Whitman's *Calamus*. 1901

4. Illustration to Whitman's *Calamus*. 1901

5. Illustration to Whitman's *Calamus*. 1901

6. Illustration to Whitman's *Calamus*. 1901

7. Studies of a New-born Babe. 1904

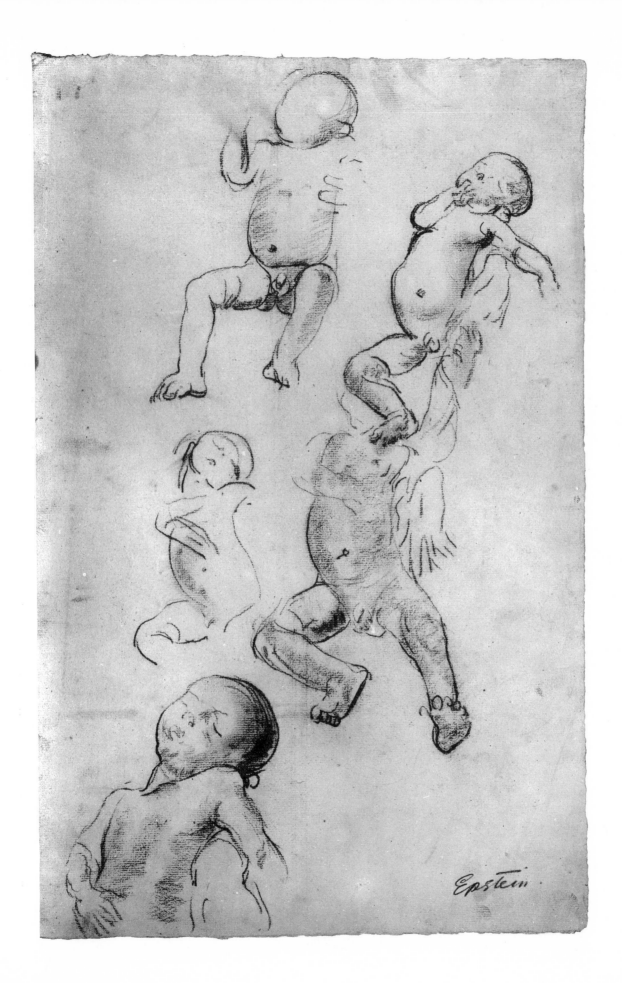

Epstein

8. Studies of a New-born Babe. 1904

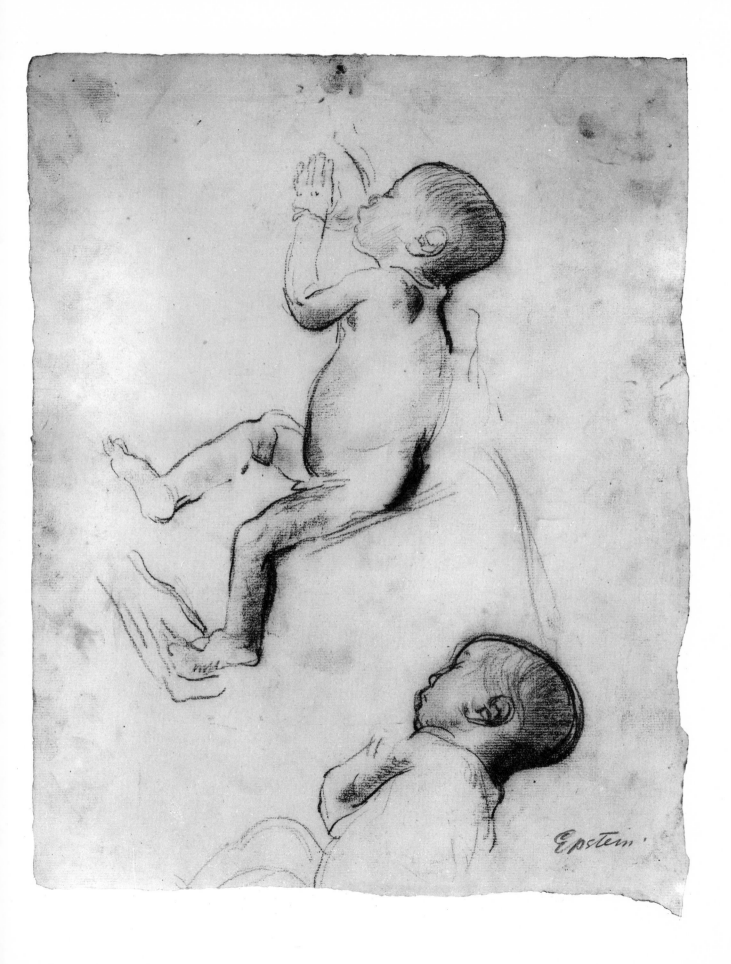

9. Profile Head of Woman. 1906

10. Woman Resting Head on Hands. 1906

11. Profile of Young Girl. 1906

44

12. Girl with a Dove. 1906

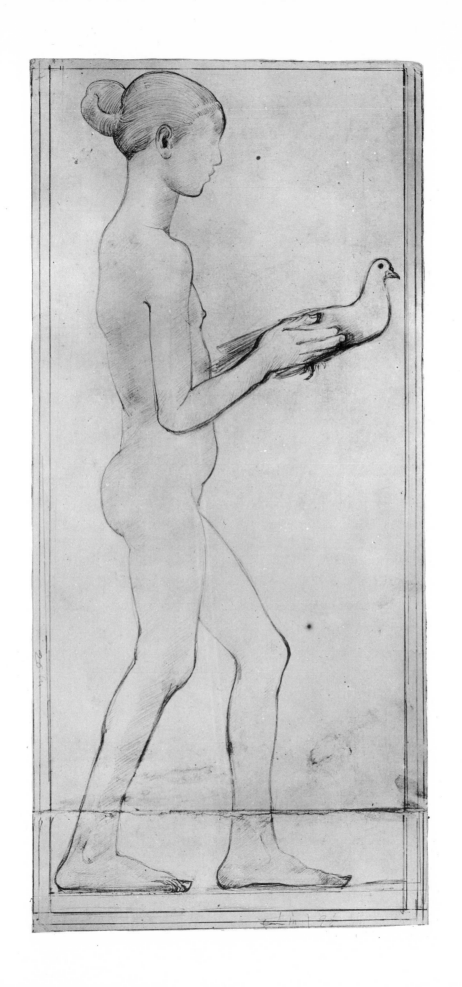

13. Mother and Child. 1907

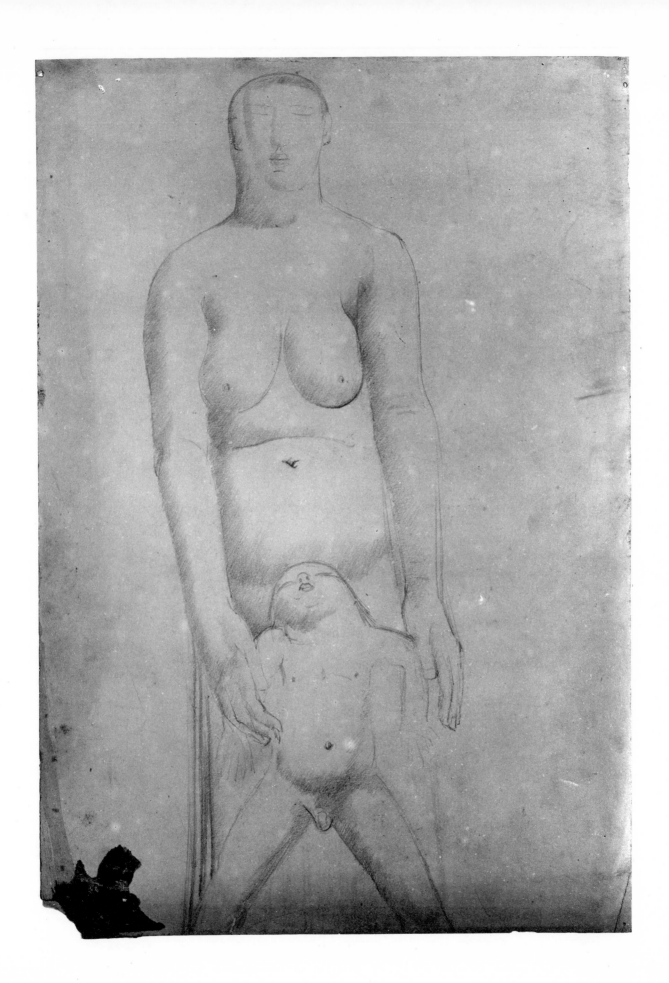

14. Hygeia, Strand Figure. 1907

Hygeia

15. Mother and Child, Strand Statue. 1907

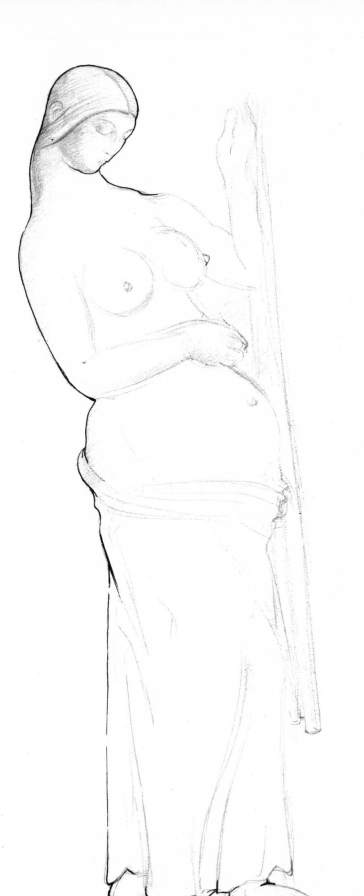

Parvati.

16. Philosopher, Studies for Strand Statue. 1907

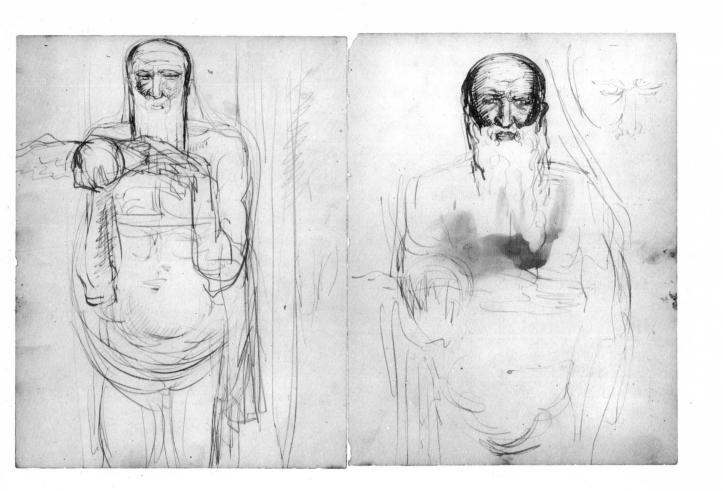

17. Profile Head, Hand and Arm. 1909

56

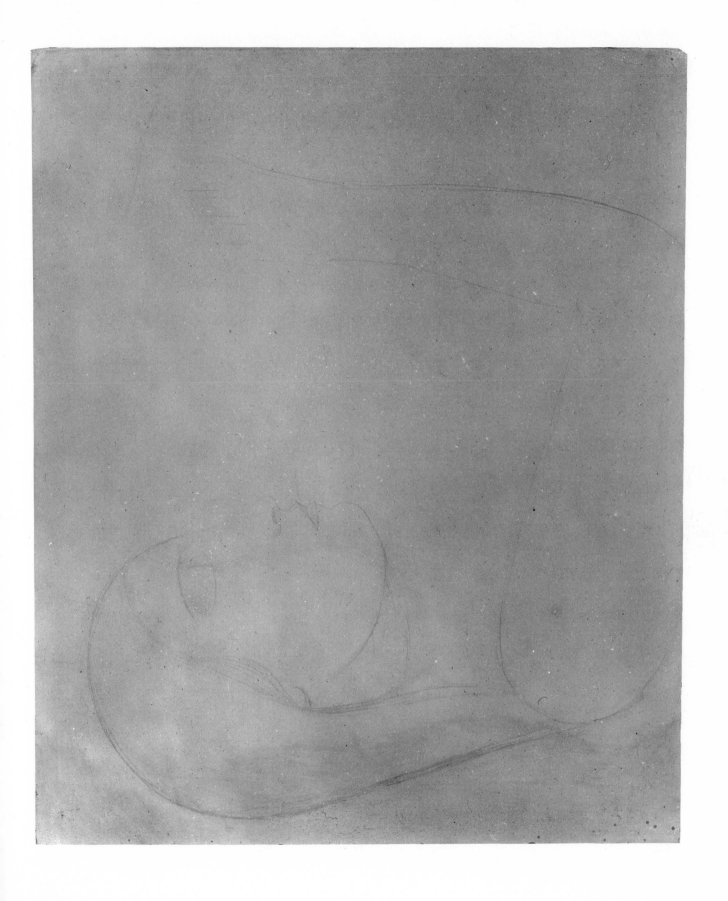

18. Hands and Arms. 1910

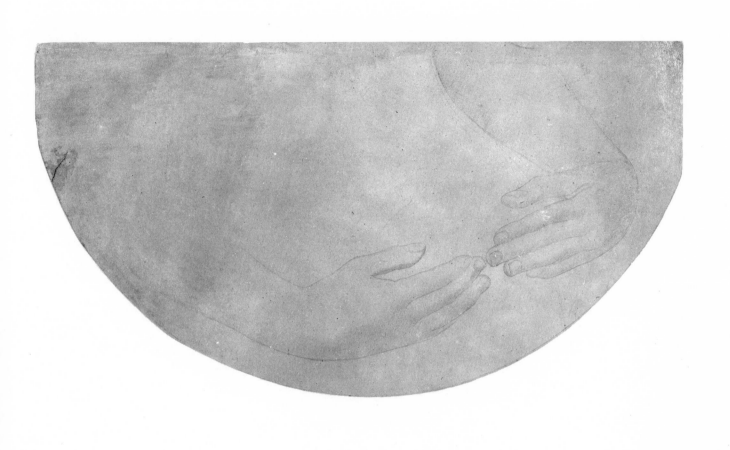

19. Study for Sculpture. Maternity. 1910

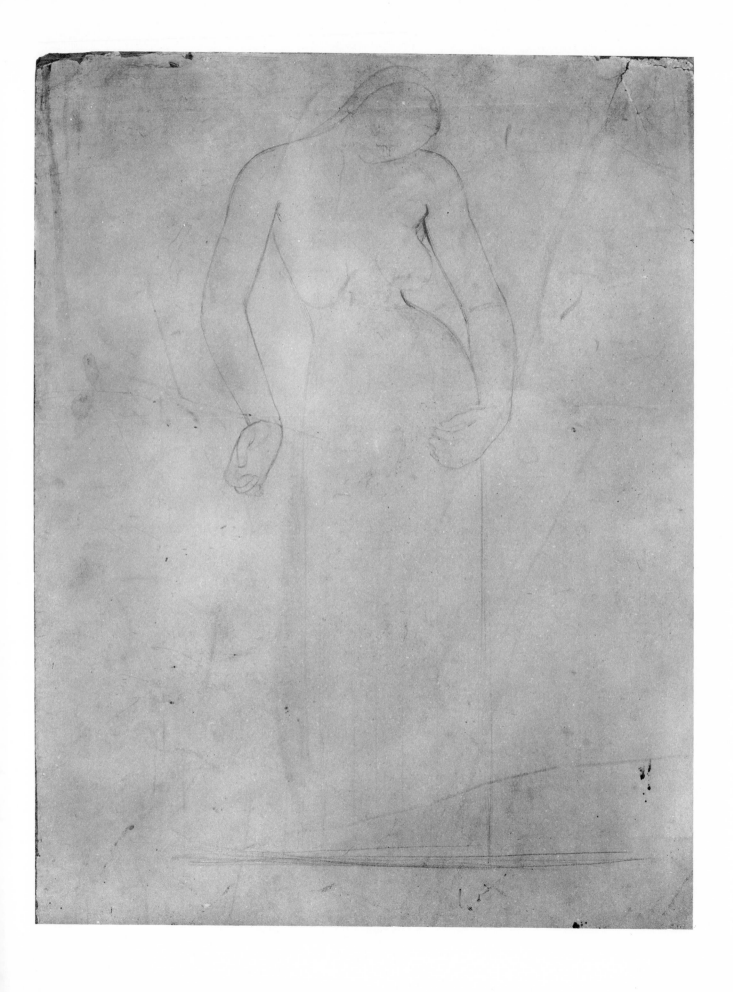

20.   Portrait Head of Young Girl. 1909

21. Portrait Head of Little Girl. 1909

22. Head of Nan. 1909

23. Two Nudes of Nan. 1911

24. Nan: Seated Nude. 1911

25. Sketch for Oscar Wilde Tomb. 1909

26. The Flame of Life. 1910

27. Vorticist Compositions. 1912

28. Sketch of Doves. 1913

29. Vorticist Figure. 1913

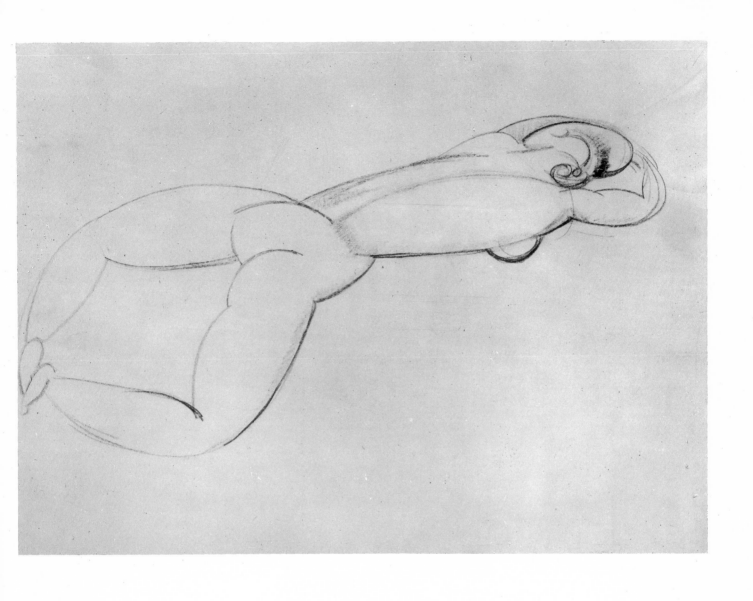

30. Head. 1913

31. Study for Rock Drill. 1915

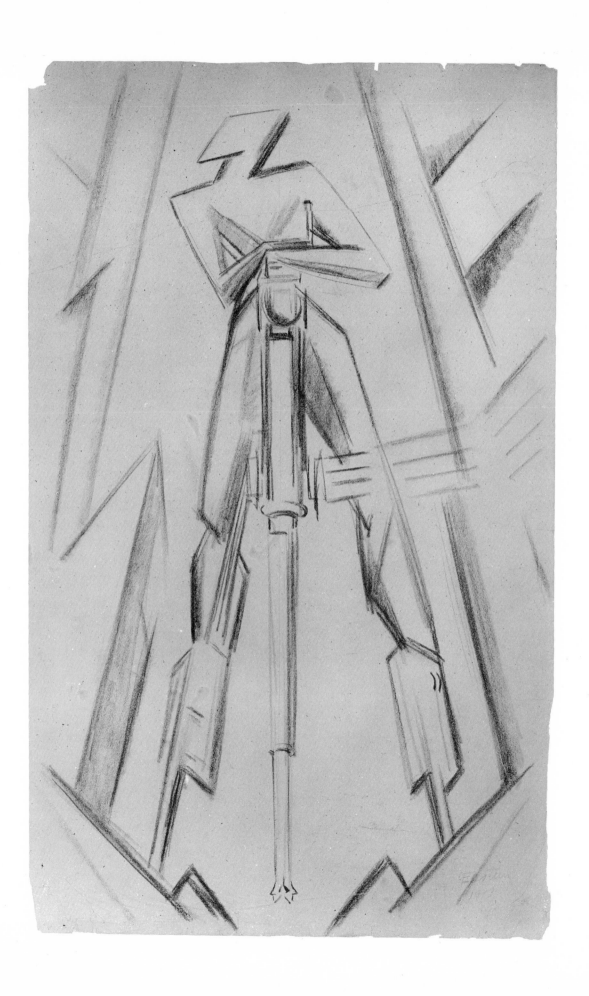

32. Study for Rock Drill: back view. 1915

Study for Rock Drill
Epstein.

33. Vorticist Composition. 1915

34. Portrait Head of a Girl. c.1916

35. Wounded Soldier. 1918

Pte. Brook
G.P. Stern.
Plymouth July 4. 1915.

36. Army Nurse. 1918

37. Study for Christ Statue. 1918

38. Portrait Head of Meum. 1918

39. Study for Fountain Group. 1918

40.   Sketch for Bas Relief, Lovers. 1922

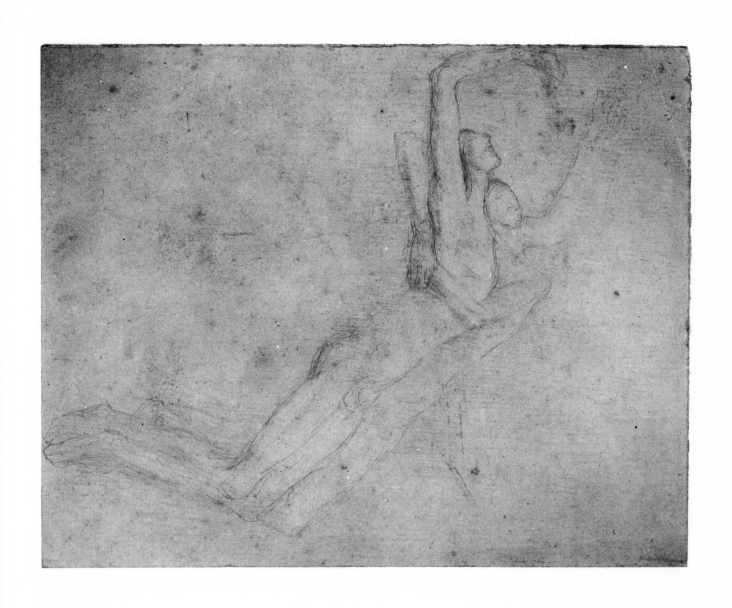

41. Song of Solomon. 1923

42. Nude of Negress. 1925

43. Head of a Negress. 1925

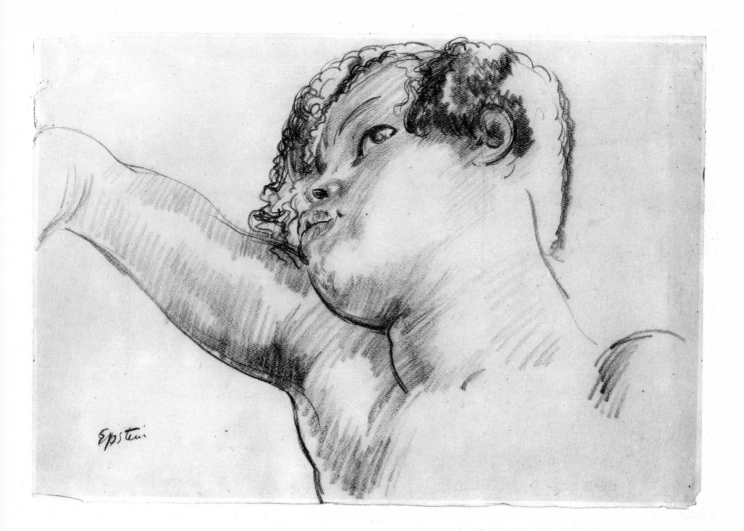

44. The Blessing. 1927

45. Figure Study, Anita. 1928

46. Study for Night. 1928

47. Head of Zeda. 1928

48. Kathleen. 1929

49. Theo. 1930

50. Noli Me Tangere. 1930

51. The Spirit Moving on the Waters. 1930

52. The Hand of God. 1930

53. Jesus and John. 1930

54. Study for Genesis. 1931

55. Pietà, Two Heads. 1932

56. Pietà, Two Figures. 1932

57. Indian Mother and Child. 1932

58. Shadrack, Meschak and Abednego. 1933

59. Figure Study, Male Nude. 1934

60. Portrait of Kitty. 1937

61. Negress Sleeping. 1938

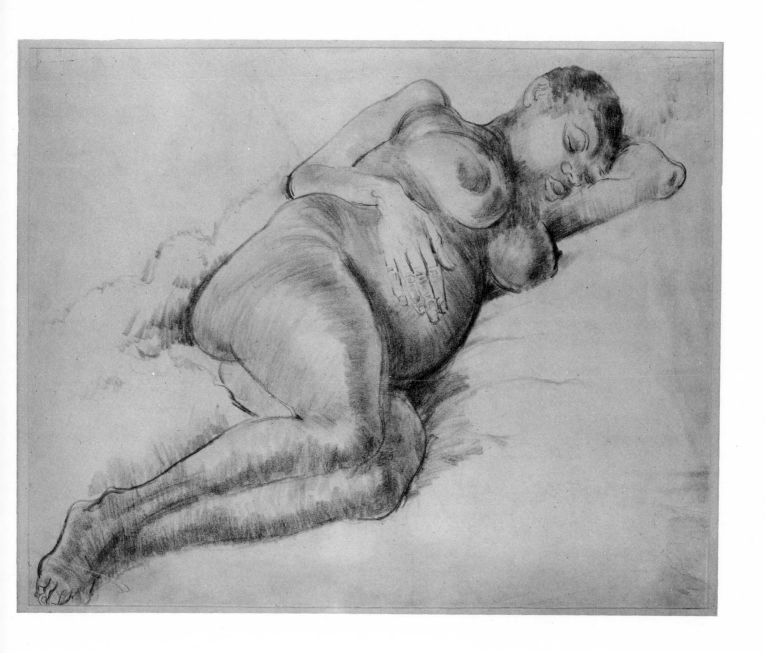

62. Illustration for Baudelaire. *La Fontaine de Sang.* 1939

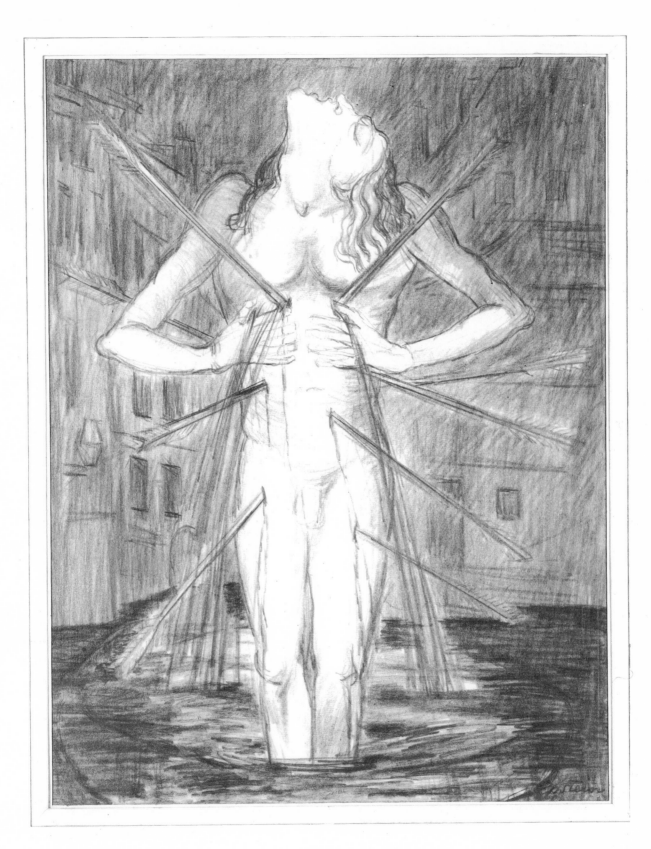

63. Lucifer and His Angels. 1944

64. Study for St. Michael Torso. 1957